My Mommy Has PTSD

Written by
Reggie, Buddy & Lia Cervantes

Illustrated by
Reggie Cervantes & Amy Marie

© 2007 Reggie, Buddy, & Lia Cervantes. All rights reserved.

No part of this book may be reproduced, stored in a retrieval system, or transmitted by any means without the written permission of the author.

This book is a work of non-fiction. Unless otherwise noted, the author and the publisher make no explicit guarantees as to the accuracy of the information contained in this book and in some cases, names of people and places have been altered to protect their privacy.

AuthorHouse™
1663 Liberty Drive
Bloomington, IN 47403
www.authorhouse.com
Phone: 1 (800) 839-8640

Because of the dynamic nature of the Internet, any web addresses or links contained in this book may have changed since publication and may no longer be valid. The views expressed in this work are solely those of the author and do not necessarily reflect the views of the publisher, and the publisher hereby disclaims any responsibility for them.

Any people depicted in stock imagery provided by Getty Images are models, and such images are being used for illustrative purposes only.
Certain stock imagery © Getty Images.

This book is printed on acid-free paper.

ISBN: 978-1-4208-0411-9 (sc)
ISBN: 978-1-4259-3076-9 (e)

Library of Congress Control Number: 2004098800

Print information available on the last page.

Published by AuthorHouse 11/08/2019

In Memory of First Lieutenant Robert (Bob) Stonehill
who passed away suddenly on August 2, 2004
and to all the other Rescue Workers who have answered the final call

My Mommy Has PTSD

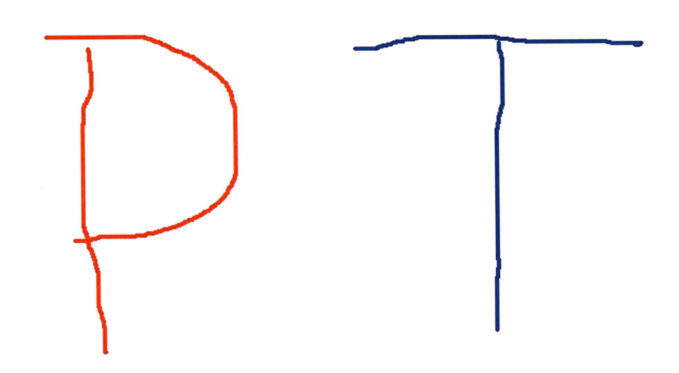

She explained to me what it means.
The P is for Post, which means after.
The T is for Traumatic, which means Terribly Scary and Dangerous.

The S is for Stress. The D is for Disorder, which means out of order. So it means that after terribly scary danger your stress puts your life out of order and life gets disorganized.

Your life changes and gets out of order and disorganized because you've been in danger.

PTSD is how people who have been in danger, like watching someone die, like when the car hit my friends mommy and she went to heaven. Not like on TV, but for real.

Mommy's PTSD is from September 11th on Ground Zero at the World Trade Center. She was a rescue worker who went to help people who were trapped or injured and needed medical attention. My mommy saw a lot of people injured and knew many died and were trapped when the buildings fell down.

My mommy gets nightmares, she can't always sleep well so she is tired a lot. That's why sometimes she gets quiet and doesn't like too much noise. She doesn't like to listen to me when she is like this. She doesn't like to talk to me when she is like this. Sometimes, I think she doesn't like me and my little brother.

She is very sad at times and doesn't let me do anything. She worries I will get into danger. She likes to be able to see me all the time.

My Mommy ↓

Mommy tried to tell me that these nightmares, tiredness, the reason she cant remember, is afraid to be in big crowds and worries about me getting into danger are the reasons and symptoms of PTSD. It's like when you have a tooth ache. It is a sign something is wrong, that's what you call a symptom.

Some of the other symptoms are that she cant handle her feelings. Some of her feelings are mixed up and are hiding.
Mommy had to hide her feelings so she could continue to work and provide for us. Being a single mommy is hard work and she needed to keep us together, so she let her feelings go into hiding.

Some of mommy's other feelings are that the things she saw come back to her all the time. These are called nightmares and flashbacks. That is why she thinks about it so much and sometimes she talks about it. She can't forget that day. She worries about being in danger and wants us to be safe.

Sometimes loud noises makes mommy jump and get scared. She use to be very jumpy but now doesn't get scared easily.

Sometimes things scare her and she reacts as if she needs to get to safety from the buildings falling around her so she doesn't get hurt.

That's why my little brother and I aren't allowed to make loud noises or sneak up on mommy.

That's why she sometimes gets angry when I don't do what she asks. You don't have time to be slow when you are in danger. You have to react she says. You have to be fast.

Sometimes when mommy has too many things going on at one time its too much for her and she yells. She doesn't realize she is yelling or is angry because her feelings are hiding.

I use to think if my brother and I were nice that maybe mommy wouldn't be so sad. If I got good grades and kept my room clean mommy would be happy again.

Sometimes when mommy is sad I get angry too. Mommy said it's because I heard so many times that she might not be coming home that night and I worried and was scared for her too. The doctors told mommy we have PTSD too.

When Mommy was at Ground Zero and knew some of the people she was friends with were dead. She didn't have time to cry. Sometimes when you cry because you are sad or hurt, you can feel better. Mommy didn't have time to cry then or after because she was too busy taking care of us. She is sometimes stuck with her feelings still hiding.

Sometimes my aunt Marie says nothing we do can erase the things mommy did that day. Like she had to run for cover and get to safety so the buildings falling wouldn't hurt her and she could come home to us.

It wasn't our fault and we cant change it says aunt Marie.

Ground Zero made mommy change and we can't change it back. Mommy has to work on it herself.

Sometimes when mommy talks about what happened in counseling and in the groups or with people when she speaks out about her work. It helps her work with her feelings that are hiding and she feels angry. We have to let her feel sad. It's okay if we are sad because mommy's sad too. Since we understand now, that it's not our fault, we can love mommy when she is sad and we don't have to be angry at her any more.

My brother, Buddy and I felt very different from our friends because we weren't allowed to do things like our friends. We are different because my mommy got her feelings hurt trying to help people. We know we didn't make mommy this way and that when she feels better we will all be happy again.

Aunt Marie says my job is to be a kid, go to school, ask questions, learn, read, make mistakes, be human, need help from grown ups and to play and be happy.

Sometimes hugs make my mommy so happy that I give her lots of them. They make me happy too.

Causes, Signs and Symptoms of PTSD

Some of the causes of PTSD are:
Act of terrorism, rape, combat, physical abuse, sexual molestation, physical attack, domestic violence, natural disasters (tornados, floods, earthquakes), explosions, life threatening situations which involve the possibility of causing death or injury.

Some of the Signs and Symptoms are:
Nightmares, flashbacks, insomnia, panic attacks, fatigue and irritability, detached, estranged, withdrawn, hyper visibility, easily startled.

Helpful Links

http://www.ncptsd.org
http://www.9-11mentalhealth.org/resources.html
http://helping.apa.org/
http://griefandrenewal.com/main.htm
your local public library

Home in Oklahoma

I awoke to the scent of summer
smoked barbecue
cloaked in sauce
a strong breeze that carried it away

I had been dreaming of pecan pie
screaming for vanilla ice cream
chocolate sauce and
two spoons to vanish it away

I was swaying in my hammock
backyard dog barking
newspaper on my lap
holding a hand in mine

It evoked a desire to dream
when I realized I was awake
it all made perfect sense
I was home in Oklahoma

About the Author

Reggie, Buddy and Lia Cervantes were deeply affected by the attacks on September 11th, at the World Trade Center.

Reggie was a Rescue Worker at Ground Zero. Her children overheard many times during the day that many firefighters, police officers and rescue workers died. The lack of communication made things difficult.

This book came about from the conversations Reggie and her daughter, Lia had with other children explaining why they didn't do things most families do. They are still recovering from their PTSD. Reggie Cervantes, like many other Rescue Workers is suffering from lung disease.

Printed in the United States
By Bookmasters